W9-AOA-086

DINOSAURS

FASCINATING FACTS

BY M. J. YORK

The Child's World®
childsworld.com

Published by The Child's World®
1980 Lookout Drive • Mankato, MN 56003-1705
800-599-READ • www.childsworld.com

Photographs ©: Shutterstock Images, cover
(*Concavenator*), cover (*Dimetrodon*), cover
(Titanosaur), cover (*T. rex*), 1 (*Concavenator*),
1 (*Dimetrodon*), 1 (Titanosaur), 1 (*T. rex*), 2,
3, 4–5, 5, 6, 7, 8, 8–9, 10, 11, 13, 14–15, 15, 16,
17, 18, 18–19, 20, 21, 24, back cover (*T. rex*),
back cover (ostrich); AP Images, 12

ISBN 9781503844667 (Reinforced Library Binding)
ISBN 9781503846210 (Portable Document Format)
ISBN 9781503847408 (Online Multi-user eBook)
LCCN 2019958002

Printed in the United States of America

ABOUT THE AUTHOR

M. J. York is a children's author
and editor living in Minnesota.
She loves learning about all
kinds of fascinating facts.

CONTENTS

INTRODUCTION

Ages ago, *Tyrannosaurus rex* (*T. rex*) shook the ground with its roar. *Triceratops* fended off the hunter with its fierce horns. Millions of years earlier, 7-foot- (2-m-) long *Coelophysis* sped after early mammals. Between *Coelophysis* and *T. rex*, scientists have discovered at least 700 strange and unique dinosaur species that stomped, leaped, and even flew.

Dinosaurs lived during the Mesozoic era. This is divided into three time periods: the Triassic, Jurassic, and Cretaceous. Dinosaurs appeared in the Triassic period, about 225 million years ago. They died out at the end of the Cretaceous period, around 66 million years ago.

Scientists are finding new dinosaurs all the time. And there are probably thousands waiting to be uncovered. The more we learn about dinosaurs, the more fascinating facts we discover.

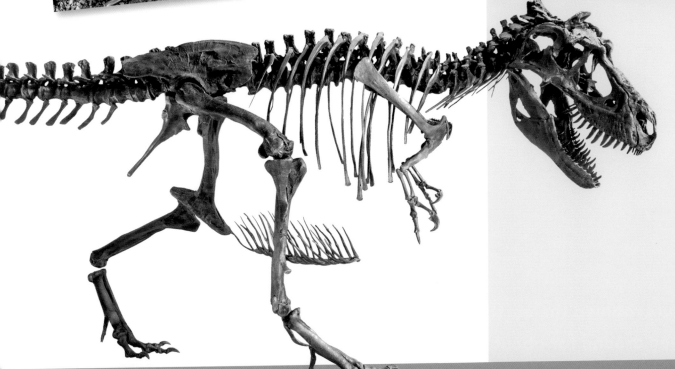

CHAPTER ONE

When Dinosaurs Roamed the Earth

Dinosaurs roamed the earth for almost 180 million years. Humans have only been around for about 300,000 years. That is 550 times as long!

66 million

◄ We are as close in time to *T. rex* as *T. rex* is to *Stegosaurus*. *T. rex* went **extinct** 66 million years ago with the rest of the dinosaurs. *Stegosaurus* went extinct 66 million years before the first *T. rex* appeared.

Dinosaurs lived on every continent on Earth, including Antarctica. At first, all the land masses were connected. They broke apart over time and moved to where they are today. Earth was also warmer than today.

The first mammals appeared around the same time as the earliest dinosaurs.

Dinosaurs were not the only ancient giant ▶ reptiles. Swimming *plesiosaurs* and winged *pterosaurs* were not dinosaurs. *Dimetrodon* was a massive **carnivorous** reptile with a large sail on its back. It lived millions of years before the first dinosaurs.

Dimetrodon
▼

Going Extinct

It took more than a gigantic **asteroid** to wipe out the dinosaurs. There is evidence that the climate was changing. There were large volcanic eruptions at the time, too. ▼

The asteroid that hit Earth exploded with the power of 10 billion nuclear bombs. The dust it threw into the air blocked the sun for years. It made a crater more than 90 miles (150 km) wide in the ocean near Mexico.

There is one dino descendant still around today: birds! Birds evolved from small cousins of *T. rex* about 145 million years ago. ▼

75%

▲

Seventy-five percent of life on Earth went extinct at the same time as the dinosaurs.

CHAPTER TWO

Weird and Wonderful

10

One tyrannosaur goes by the nickname "Pinocchio rex." It is called this because of its long, crocodile-like nose.

◄ *T. rex* swallowed all of its food whole. Its **serrated** teeth were as long as bananas. The teeth were good for slicing through prey, but not for chewing.

Spinosaurus was the largest carnivore, even bigger than *T. rex*. It is the only known dinosaur that spent most of its life in water. It had a sail on its back that was taller than most people.

Therizinosaurs were odd-looking relatives of *T. rex*. This group of dinosaurs had feathers, long necks and arms, and gigantic claws on their hands. Despite their scary look, they ate plants, not meat.

The largest dinosaur with feathers was *Yutyrannus huali*. It weighed 1.5 tons (1.4 metric tons), and its name means "beautiful feathered tyrant."

▲

From the neck up, *Concavenator* looked like a regular **theropod**. But scientists believe unusual tufts of feathers sprouted from its elbows. And weirdest of all, a triangular hump poked up in the middle of its back.

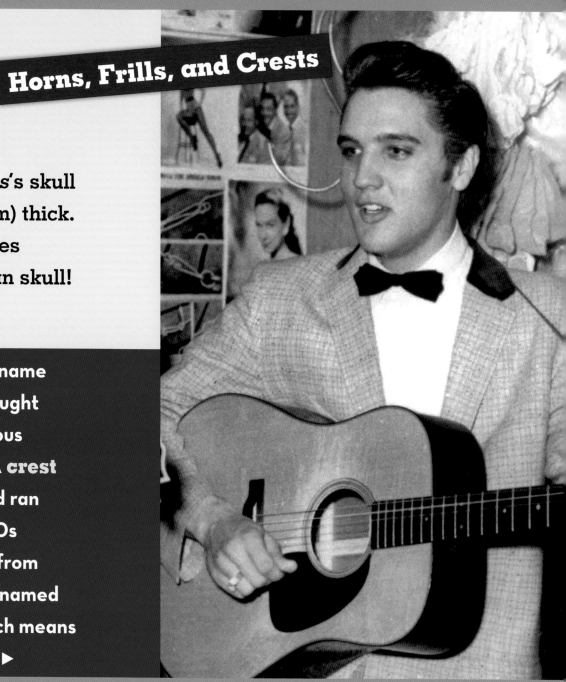

Pachycephalosaurus's skull was 10 inches (25 cm) thick. That is about 40 times thicker than a human skull!

Elvisaurus got its nickname because someone thought it looked like the famous singer, Elvis Presley. A **crest** on the dinosaur's head ran side to side like a 1950s hairdo. This dinosaur from Antarctica is actually named *Cryolophosaurus*, which means "cold-crested lizard." ▶

12

Amargasaurus was the punk rock dinosaur. It looked like it had a mohawk! This **sauropod** had a double row of spines or possibly two sails running down its neck. ▶

Kosmoceratops might win the prize for having the most spikes and frills. Related to *Triceratops*, this dinosaur had spikes on its face and a big frill with a fringe of more spikes hanging down.

The Dragon King of Hogwarts (*Dracorex hogwartsia*) is a dinosaur skeleton that has a bony skull that looks like a dragon. Visitors to a children's museum in Indiana voted on its name. Scientists are unsure if it is a new species or a young *Pachycephalosaurus*.

13

CHAPTER THREE

Biggest, Fastest, Tallest, Smallest

The largest dinosaurs were as long as a ▶ jumbo-jet wing. Titanosaurs were a type of sauropod, with four legs and long necks and tails. The biggest might have been 120 feet (37 m) long, the largest land animals ever.

14

A *Brachiosaurus* heart weighed about 440 pounds (200 kg). This let it pump blood 26 feet (8 m) up the long neck to the brain.

Some of the biggest dinosaurs had the smallest brains. *Ampelosaurus* was 50 feet (15 m) long, but like other sauropods, its brain was only the size of a walnut.

440 pounds

The *Mamenchisaurus* had a neck that was stretched to the extreme. Its neck was more than 35 feet (11 m) long, or about the length of a school bus. This was more than half its length. Its neck was longer for its size than any other dinosaur.

A baby sauropod gained 10 times its weight in just over six weeks. Born the size of a human baby, it reached more than 80 pounds (36 kg) in a few weeks!

Microraptor had four ▶ wings! Each limb had feathers like a bird. It was smaller than a chicken, making it one of the smallest dinosaurs. Its name means "tiny plunderer," and it ate insects and small animals.

16

The tyrannosaur *Dilong*, a small relative of *T. rex*, weighed only 25 pounds (11 kg). It lived 60 million years earlier.

3 pounds

▲

Aquilops was a tiny ancestor of the huge horned *Triceratops*. It weighed only 3 pounds (1.4 kg).

Linhenykus was a small theropod that could sit on your lap. It had tiny arms with just one finger each, ending in a claw. Scientists think it used them to dig for bugs.

The smallest sauropod was the size of an ox. Called *Europasaurus*, it was about one-fifth as long as its giant cousins, *Apatosaurus* and *Diplodocus*.

▼

One of the smallest dinosaurs had the longest name! *Micropachycephalosaurus* means "tiny thick-headed lizard." It was related to *Pachycephalosaurus*. It had a bony skull like its larger cousins but was only 2 feet (0.6 m) long.

Stronger, Faster, Smarter

Ornithomimus was probably the fastest dinosaur. The name means "bird mimic," and it looked and ran a lot like a modern ostrich. With long and powerful legs, it reached 50 miles per hour (80 km/h), a little faster ◄ than today's big birds. ▼

50
miles per hour

Troodon had one of the biggest dinosaur brains. But this human-sized dino's brain was the size of an opossum's, making it no competition for ultra-smart mammals.

T. rex had the strongest bite of any land animal. Its bite was ten times as forceful as an alligator's bite. But megalodon, an ancient shark, could bite three times harder than *T. rex*.

▼

The fastest big predator was *Carnotaurus*. *Carnotaurus* had tiny arms, even smaller than *T. rex*. But its huge, powerful legs made it super speedy. It was also the only theropod with horns.

Maiasauras were some of the best dinosaur parents. They lived in herds, made nests, and cared for their babies.

CHAPTER FOUR

Fantastic Fossil Finds

On average, scientists describe a new type of dinosaur every ten days! ▶

20

We can discover the skin or feather color of some dinosaurs. If a fossil is very ▲ well preserved, scientists sometimes find microscopic **pigment** in the rock. Then, they can match the patterns of pigment onto the animal's body.

At Dinosaur National Monument in Colorado, you can see 1,500 fossils sticking out of a cliff wall. It is part of the Carnegie Quarry, one of the largest sites of Jurassic fossils in the world.

The Dueling Dinosaurs were found in Montana in 2006. The *Triceratops* and *T. rex* apparently died while fighting, locked in combat for millions of years. A similar fighting *Velociraptor* and *Protoceratops* were found in Mongolia in 1971.

Scientists who found *Oviraptor* in the 1920s thought they had discovered a crime scene. *Oviraptor* looked like it was stealing eggs from another dinosaur, so they named it "egg thief." Later research showed *Oviraptor* was actually the parent of the eggs. It was protecting them, not trying to eat them.

Glossary

asteroid (AS-tuh-royd) An asteroid is a rock that is smaller than a planet that orbits the sun. A big asteroid hit Earth 66 million years ago.

carnivorous (kar-NIV-ur-uhs) An animal that is carnivorous eats mostly meat. Many dinosaurs were carnivorous.

crest (KREST) A dinosaur crest is a bony part that sticks out from its skull. A crest might look like a tube or a fan.

extinct (ik-STINGKT) A species that is extinct is no longer living on Earth. Dinosaurs went extinct 66 million years ago.

pigment (PIG-munt) Pigment is a material that gives something color. Pigment left in fossils tells scientists about dinosaur skin colors.

sauropod (SORE-uh-pod) A sauropod was a large, four-legged dinosaur with a small head and long neck and tail. One well-known sauropod is *Brachiosaurus*.

serrated (ser-AY-tid) Something that is serrated has a blade with teeth like a saw. The *T. rex* had serrated teeth.

theropod (THAYR-uh-pod) A theropod was a two-legged, meat-eating dinosaur that usually had small arms. One famous theropod is *T. rex*.

To Learn More

In the Library

Rooney, Anne. *Dinosaur Atlas*. New York, NY: Lonely Planet Kids, 2017.

Weird But True! Dinosaurs. Washington, DC: National Geographic Kids, 2020.

Woodward, John. *The Dinosaur Book*. New York, NY: DK Publishing, 2018.

On the Web

Visit our website for links about dinosaurs:

childsworld.com/links

Note to Parents, Teachers, and Librarians: We routinely verify our Web links to make sure they are safe and active sites. So encourage your readers to check them out!

Index